by Kaisen Iguchi

translated by
John Clark

CONTENTS

Cover Photo: A Standard Tea Kettle

TEA CEREMONY

by Kaisen Iguchi
translated by John Clark

© All rights reserved. No.31 of Hoikusha's Color Books Series.Published by Hoikusha Publishing Co., Ltd., 8-6, 4-chome, Tsurumi, Tsurumi-ku, Osaka,538 Japan. ISBN 4-586-54031-1. First Edition in 1975. 17th Edition in 1996. Printed in JAPAN

Tea house at Urasenke 'Yu-in'

Interior of a tea room with a skylight

THE TEA ROOM

Before the 15th century tea used to be served in part of a large reception room closed off by a screen. In the Muromachi period, however, Ashikaga Yoshimasa built the first tea room. This was a four and a half mat room called Dojinsai built into a corner of the Togudo Hall beside his own Silver Pavilion. This was the inception of the tea room, but towards the end of the 16th century, Takeno Jo-o built a four and a half mat room which had a straw roof in imitation of a farm house. He constructed it as a separate building in the middle of which he cut a space for the brazier. In later periods tea rooms of different sizes were constructed on this four and a half mat plan.

Bamboo middle ▶
gate

ROJI — the dewy path

The tea room is usually built apart from other buildings in one corner of the roji. This runs through the garden belonging to the tea room and is separated into an inner and outer roji which are distinguished by the middle gate. Since the outer roji is near to the waiting arbour, a roofed waiting bench is constructed outside. The guests wait for each other in the arbour and, when their numbers are completed, they walk along the roji to the waiting bench where they attend on the host. When preparations are completed in the tea room, the host opens the middle gate from the inner roji and greets the guests wordlessly with a single bow. The guests respond by arising from the waiting bench and wordlessly making a single bow. They watch the host return along the inner roji and then continue along it themselves one at a time. The last guest passes through the middle gate and shuts it.

◀ Roofed middle gate

When walking along the roji the guests must be careful only to proceed over the stepping stones one at a time and not to step on the ground, especially the moss. The distance between the guests must not get too narrow.

Roji sandals, which have been double-braided in a bamboo sheath, are worn when walking along the path. In rainy weather clogs of straight-grained red cedar are worn, to which the bamboo sheath is attached by a thong. The guests walk along the roji avoiding the rain by carrying a roji umbrella in one hand, which is usually made of straight sheaths of bamboo.

The middle gate

These are usually simple affairs with a gate of intertwined bamboo hung between two stakes on either side of the roji. But there are also gates with roofs and two-leafed plank doors. The various forms including the plum-viewing and umbrella-lattice gates, vary according to the preference of the host and the air he wishes to give to the roji.

The word roji originates from Buddhist sutras where it indicates a spotless place, and thus the middle gate marks the precincts of the inner roji which is a still more pure place.

Layout of the dewy path

In general, the outer roji is not over-picturesque and has an air of purity, whilst, on entering the inner roji, it is normal for the tone of elegant simplicity and mysterious depth to be strengthened. This scenery is composed of the middle gate, a stone lantern, and a stone wash-basin. Flowering trees are avoided in the roji since it is best to grow evergreen trees. The exception is however related of Rikyu's grandson, Sotan, who grew cherry trees in the roji.

Stepping stones

The crossing stones arranged in the roji are the most important aspects of its scenery, so a natural stone is employed with a flat upper surface.

◀ Stepping stones and 'detaining' stone

The guests' preparation room

Above all, the placement of stones should facilitate crossing the roji, so Rikyu teaches that 'Crossing is six parts, scenery is four parts critical', the stones being arranged so as to produce a natural effect. The arrangement may be of the kind often called 'cross-stiched' where the appearance of the scenery is enhanced by the asymmetric placement of the stones.

In the Senke School stones are, as a rule, placed at a height of 6 centimetres above the ground, but in other schools they are also placed at heights of 4.5 and 3 centimetres. Once when Rikyu was invited to the tea ceremony of his son Doan, he grumbled, on walking along the roji, that 'this stone is a little high', and, on his return, he noticed that it had been adjusted. The height of the stones is quite as delicate as this story indicates.

'Plank' stones ▶

8

'Bean shower' stones

Late in his life Sotan passed on the Fushin-an house to his third son, Sosa. In the back garden he built the houses Yu-in, Konnichi-an and Kanun-tei, to which he retired. The placement of the stones in the roji of the Yu-in house was uninteresting, and Sotan, having considered the problem a little, finally scattered several stones haphazardly like a shower of beans. Even if he had tried to place them artlessly, in the event the stepping stones were tastefully arranged. For, even though the stones appear to be placed artlessly, on closer examination there is no superfluity in the size of the stones or the interval between them, and the harmony attained is suitable for a hermitage. I think they reveal the dignity of Sotan who spent his life wholeheartedly in a natural and unaffected way of tea.

Stone wash-basin

This is placed in the inner roji near the tea room at a low height so that the guest may crouch and use the water before entering the tea room. It ensures that the guest carries a feeling of humility into the tea room — as if he had rinsed his mouth and washed his hands in the clear waters springing from the rocks of a mountain temple.

In front of the wash-basin is the stones on which the guest crouches to use the water. To the left is the stone on which a bucket filled with hot water is placed during winter. To the right is the stone on which a candlestick is placed for evening tea ceremonies. The water in the wash-basin was brought and filled by the host himself. However, there are also basins where the water falls through a water pipe which has been set up in replica of a mountain landscape.

Stone wash-basin with a tilting water spout

Stone wash-basin

'Detaining' stone

Whilst this is one of the items of roji landscape, it may sometimes be overlooked because of its small size. Round stones exactly the size of a fist are bound with bracken cord in the shape of a cross, and are placed on the stepping-stones in several places. These stepping-stones make up a single path even if they have been laid down in a meandering pattern. However, stepping-stones may also have been laid down in different directions to that of the main path. The detaining stone is placed on top of the stepping-stone which divides the path and acts as a sign that the guest must not go beyond that stone. In the past there were barrier gates on the Hokuriku and Tokai highroads at which people wishing to pass along the road were subject to investigation. The official at the barrier was the 'detainer', who is sung of in Waka poetry. Since the word was employed by men of culture, it probably also came to be applied in the way of tea to the stone which seals off a path.

'Detaining' stone

Waste container

This is a rectangular hole compacted from mortar which has been constructed at ground level at the end of the tea room eaves. Long chopsticks of young bamboo are placed in it on a convenient stone in a corner. Rectangular waste holes are constructed for tea rooms of more than four and a half mats, whilst circular holes are made for smaller rooms. The waste hole is in ordinary language called a 'rubbish' disposal hole, in fact 'rubbish' is not discarded into it. It is rather built as one of the items of roji landscape.

Waste container ▶

Stone lantern

The stone lantern may not be omitted as an item of roji landscape. It is generally placed at a low height to illuminate the footsteps of guests at evening tea ceremonies.

A paper screen is inserted in the window of the lantern flame box, but it is taken out during the day and is re-inserted when the flame is lit at night.

There are various forms of stone lanterns, many of which have special names. The photograph shows the Oribe lantern at Kitano Shrine, Kyoto (see the right page). It is renowned as the Maria lantern reputedly liked by Oribe Furuta because there is an image of the Virgin Mary carved into the upright. Stone lanterns were originally made to provide light for shrines and Buddhist pavilions. Their forms and names can

Snow-viewing stone lantern (Kanshu-ji)

generally be distinguished into the Nara and Kyoto styles, in the variation of which the preference of the tea master lies.

The Nara styles are those of the Tachibana, Hannya, Tonomine and Ganko Temples. The Kyoto styles are those of Uzumasa, Yawata, Byodoin, Yukimi and that of Daitoku-ji Temple.

The tea masters Shuko, Jo-o, Rikyu, Oribe, Yuraku, Enshu, and Sowa are famous in their preferences for stone lanterns. There is a famous story of Rikyu who chipped a piece from the umbrella top of his own stone lantern because it was too well finished. This lantern survives today as the memorial tower of Hosokawa Tadaoki in the Koto-in sub-temple of Daitoku-ji.

Oribe stone lantern
(Kitano Shrine)

15

The guests' small entrance

An entry constructed in the tea house where the guests enter and leave on their knees. The word 'pass under' is written in an old tea book, which later became 'crawl up' and was then further abbreviated to 'crawling'. The size of the entrance is not necessarily fixed but the criterion has become one of about 66 centimetres high by 60 centimetres wide. However, the guests' 'crawling' entrance at the Tai-an tea house is larger than usual. This was built by

'Crawling' entrance

Rikyu at Myoki-an, Yamazaki, Kyoto Prefecture at the command of Hideyoshi on the occasion of the Battle of Yamazaki in June, 1582. This door was larger than usual so that it was possible to enter the tea house wearing armour.

A plank door is inserted in the 'crawling' entrance. Guests crouch on the stone where they take off their shoes, open the plank door, and enter the tea room crawling with the head lowered. Such a small entrance was constructed to set a partition between the tea room and the ordinary world outside and

16

Decorative broom

to provide for a feeling of humility at the moment the guest's head was lowered.

The 'crawling' entrance was devised by Rikyu. It was recorded in the tea book 'Matsuya Diary' that 'Rikyu began to use the crawling entrance in a small tea room, remembering his fascination with the crawling exit he had experienced on the boat from Osaka to Hirakata.'

A broom is hung from the pillar of the 'crawling' entrance. This is of disentangled bracken thongs bound to a handle of green bamboo and is always hung outside tea rooms which have a waste hole. There is also a hemp palm broom of five young hemp palm leaves tied in a bunch and fastened to a green bamboo handle by wisteria vines. It is hung on the pillar of the bench in the waiting arbour of the outer roji. These two brooms are not simply decorative, for leaves sometimes fall onto the beautiful cleanly swept roji. If there are such fallen leaves when the host comes out to greet the guests, they are swept up with this brush and discarded into the waste hole.

Peeping in on the host in the guise of sweeping up leaves is also one of the aesthetic delights of the tea ceremony.

TEA UTENSILS

The different kinds of utensils used in the tea ceremony first came from China. When its etiquette was not yet established, these utensils were tea bowls, flower containers, and hanging scrolls. However, when the etiquette of the tea ceremony was laid down by Murata Shuko in the period of the Ashikaga Yoshimasa (15th century), several other utensils became necessary. Various implements from China were used until Takeno Jo-o developed a tea ceremony with an aesthetic of simplicity towards the end of the 16th century. Utensils made in Japan were then changed to from those made in China.

Tenmoku or celadon tea bowls had been used but then they became wares made in Seto and Bizen. Flower containers likewise had been Chinese bronze vessels, but then changed to tubes made of bamboo, and wares fired in Iga, like Shiga-raki, came to be used. Tea containers were originally small pots which, in China, were filled with medicines or seasoning and these again were made in Seto or thereabouts.

Other essential implements all came to be made domestically and this was the cause for the diffusion of the tea ceremony even among the ordinary people. Yet the different kinds of utensils brought from China were not thrown away. They were called 'Chinese things', were highly valued and used in the decoration of the stand for tea utensils in special tea ceremonies. Works by the brush of high Chinese monks were especially esteemed as hanging scrolls, which taste extends to the present day.

Decoration of the stand for tea utensils

Stand for tea utensils

   This is the highest form of decoration used in the way of tea. The stand is a shelf on four legs of black lacquer which crossed from China as a utensils of the Zen Sect at the end of the Kamakura period (13th century). Is is formal procedure to place the kettle for a portable brazier in the middle of the stand and to ornament the stand with a water jar of Chinese bronze, a standing scoop, a waste-water container and a lid rest. In later years ceramics of the Ninsei style with its decoration in coloured enamels were made in place of Chinese

19

Tea ceremony in the reception room

bronze. The top of the stand is ornamented with a tea jar, but sometimes an incense container or a feather brush is displayed instead.

A tea stand cannot be used in a tea room of less than four and a half mats. If the decoration of a tea stand is taken as the formal (shin) style, then the method of decoration where the kettle for a portable brazier is deployed in a small room may be ranked as the informal (so) style. In the latter case tea is made in the style of natural simplicity.

In the tea ceremony which takes place in a large room or a reception room, sumptuous utensils are used. Here beside hanging scrolls and flower vases, incense containers and other small things are also displayed in the decoration of the alcove. In the side alcove are displayed utensils for the incense ceremony and a silver lacquered inkstone box, or books of old poems and horizontal scrolls.

The hanging scrolls are sometimes called 'poetry fragments' in which part of a collection of poems has been made into a scroll. Or sometimes the paper napkin brought to hold cakes during the ceremony has had a poem written on it and this has subsequently been made into a scroll. For the flower container a celadon or old copper vessel is used.

The 'informal' (so) tea ceremony

Hanging scrolls

When Kanpaku Hidetsugu returned with the duck cloth painting boards (shikishi) he had ordered in the province of Tsukushi, he decided to hold a tea ceremony to which he invited Rikyu together with two or three other guests.

"It was about the 21st of April when the dawn tea party was held. There was not even an oil lamp by the seats and only the sound of the kettle bubbling was heard : it was exceptionally tranquil. After we had taken our places the screen behind us slowly and dimly got brighter..... Rikyu suddenly stood up and opened it. From that moment the sinking daybreak moon in the West lit up the window, and, as he looked at the hanging scroll by its light, a poem by Fujiwara Teika was read: 'If you look towards the singing cuckoo, only the daybreak moon remains'." The fascination of the tea ceremony lied in a moment such as this.

Poetry fragment ▶

Fragments of old poems

These are hanging scrolls made up from a section cut from the text of a sutra or from an old collection of poems. They are named after their contents and also after the title of the collection or the name of the author. These are mostly from before the end of the Kamakura period (14th century) and are seen as the best of their kind by men of tea.

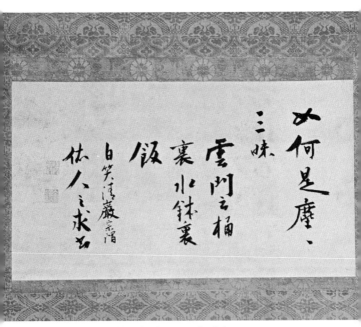

Calligraphy fragment by Seigan

Poems of a single line

These are hanging scrolls with characters written vertically in a single line. There are as well recent single line poems among the calligraphs used in the ceremony. However, apart from the old calligraphs, tea men most delight in one line poems by the brush of the head of a tea school. There are many of these from about the time of Rikyu's grandson Sotan, but there are probably no one line poems by the brush of Rikyu himself.

There are many Zen epigrams among the contents of the single line poems, and also lines from the ancient poetry of China. Men of tea are not concerned about the skill with which the characters were written, but show interest in the contents of the phrases. Then, tea men give their hearts to the writer of the poem in trying to get a little closer to the spirit of tea embraced by the men of old.

◀ One line calligraphy by Sotan

Laudatory poems written above a painting

These are hanging scrolls painted by someone else in praise of which a tea man has written a poem above. They may also be scrolls of paintings done for pleasure by a tea man above which appropriate phrases were written. Pictures using colour done by the hand of a professional painter are not hung in the tea room. There are times however when ink paintings by Sesshu or Tanyu and such like are hung in the tea room.

Paintings by the brush of tea men are mostly unskilful ink paintings, because tea men are not professional painters. Yet the laudatory poems written above even such unskilful pictures produce a fascination which can also be thought of as resembling Zen enlightenment. There is therefore no value in such a scroll if there is discord between the painting and the laudatory poem. Such scrolls are not for formal use like old calligraphs, and consequently are best hung up when thin powdered tea is served.

Painting with laudatory poem ▶

Blue and white
water jar

Coloured enamel
water jar

Nikko bucket

Water jar of plain
curved wood

Water jars

These are always kept in the tea room filled with water
to wash the tea bowl and to make good the hot water in the
tea kettle.

In earlier times bronze vessels brought from China were
employed, but from the era of Jo-o, wares fired in Bizen and
Shiga-raki came to be used. These had formerly been employed
as seed and salt jars in farm houses, and were in the beginning used as water jars in the tea ceremony. Rikyu, however,

used a water jar made from the plain curved wood of red cedar in order to give the tea room an air of purity. Even today a water jar of curved wood is used at the initiation ceremony of a tea school. Rikyu also liked water jars in the form of a lacquered hand bucket and a plain wooden well bucket. This was probably to bring out a feeling of purity.

In the period after Rikyu celadon and blue-and-white water jars were used which had been made to order in China. Pots from Holland and water or wine jars of unglazed pottery from the South, called 'Southern Barbarian' wares were also used as water containers. In the Edo period Nonomura Ninsei began to make beautiful coloured enamel ceramics. These are, however, not used with thick powdered tea. Ceramic water jars may also be distinguished into those where both the body and the lid are the same, and jars where the lid only is painted.

There are occasions where the water jar is placed on a shelf and some where it is placed dir ctly on the rice mat floor. In the latter case the host moves out the water jar just before he begins to make tea. Since the water jar is large and difficult to move, it is put down in a place decided beforehand, and is called the 'placed water jar'. Water jars fired with rough clay like Iga ware are not displayed on a shelf, but are moved out during the ceremony or earlier put in the allotted place. In summer and when it is hot, a jar with a broad flat mouth is used. When the lid is removed, it can be seen to be full of water so that the guests may feel cool.

Almost unglazed wares are used after immersion in water, jars of plain curved wood also being immersed. In the case of earthenware, the colour of the clay may be more beautifully perceived, and, in the case of plain wood, a greater sense of purity may be felt.

Ceramic tea caddies

The Zen priest, Eisai, brought tea with him when he returned from China. He sent some of it in a small jar to the monk, Myoe of Kozan-ji Temple, at Toganoo in Kyoto. Since the jar had exactly the same shape as the persimmons in the Imperial Palace, it was called 'persimmon stem' and has become the basic shape for all tea caddies. The original tea caddies themselves probably crossed from China too, but later they were fired in Seto, Bizen et cetera. Nevertheless, Chinese tea caddies were still highly prized by men of tea.

The shape of the tea caddy has various forms. There are high-shouldered, round, bulge-bottom, gourd-shaped and other patterns of which the general shape is that of the high-shouldered caddy.

Bag for tea caddy (Shifuku) **High-shouldered (Kata-tsuki)** **Bulbous (Taikai)**

Bag for tea caddy   Tea caddy   Tea caddy in a bag

Ceramic tea caddies have an ivory lid to the reverse side of which gold paper is pasted. In the past this gold paper was replaced each time guests were welcomed, but nowadays in contrast the old colour is appreciated.

Tea caddies are kept in a bag made from old silk fragments called a shifuku. The caddy is filled with thick powdered tea, put away in the bag, and displayed in front of the water jar. In making tea the bag is removed and a napkin is folded with which the caddy is wiped. When, at the end of the ceremony, the tea caddy is put back in its silk bag, it is then put in a special box which is in turn inserted in a further bag and the whole placed in an outer box.

1	2	3	4

1. Flat and wide (Hira-natsume) 2. Round (Maru-natsume)
3. Middle-sized (Chu-natsume)   4. Gourd shaped (Hisagogata)

Ceramic tea caddies are containers for thick powdered tea, but thin powdered tea is put in a container generally called an usuki, of which the usual type is called a natsume, or jujube-shaped vessel.

The natsume type is so called because it actually resembles the jujube, a plum-like fruit. These are divided according to size into large, medium and small, the large size being further subdivided into large and medium. In general, distinction into the three types large, medium and small will suffice.

The formal type of natsume is of pure lacquer, that is painted with black lacquer. In the Edo period, however, inlay lacquer caddies were made. These were, at first, unprominently inlaid with lacquer of the same colour, but they became more extravagant and were made with a raised gold inlay on a previously laid ground of sprinkled gold. There were, moreover, not only natsume of pure lacquer, but also those made with cinnabar, with very thin lacquer coating so that the wood grain showed through, and with a very thin but brilliant lacquer.

Natsume also have various shapes. The 'chamfered-edge' shape has a flat top to its lid and a depressed edge. The 'snowdrift' shape has chamfered edges on both the lid and the base and is so called because the top and bottom cannot be distinguished, the same as being unable to tell the way in a snowdrift.

Snowdrift
(Fubuki-natsume)

Chamfered edge
(Mentori-natsume)

1. Middle-sized (Chu-natsume)
2. Flat and wide (Hira-natsume)
3. Red lid with black body (Koaka-natsume)

There is a low flat natsume, and a 'tortoiseshell' natsume which has a red lid with a black body. 'Tortoiseshell' is, in fact, the name for the upper part of the natsume lid which is wiped with a napkin during the preparation of tea.

There are many natsume which have been liked by generations of heads of tea schools. To these specific names have been given, even among natsume of the same medium shape. There is, for example, a caddy with inlaid cherry blossoms among the class of pure lacquer black natsume. This is called the 'evening cherry' natsume.

1. formal
2. normal
3. informal

Tea scoops

These are spoon-like utensils for ladling out powdered tea. They were at first made of ivory, but, from the time of Takeno Jo-o, came to be made of whittled bamboo. Those made of bamboo are distinguished into those with a joint in the centre, at the bottom, and those without a joint. Thus scoops of ivory and bamboo scoops without a joint are ranked as formal scoops, and those whose joint is at the bottom are ranked as standard scoops. Informal scoops are the ones usually employed, and they also include scoops made from woods other than bamboo, such as twigs of plum and pine.

Tea scoops are whittled by tea men themselves and put in a bamboo tube on which the name is written. The name used is appropriate to the tea man's preference in the surface staining of bamboo and his state of mind at the time he whittled out the scoop.

Tea scoop and
their containing tube ▶

Flat tea bowls as used with a portable brazier

Tea bowls

In the earliest period of the tea ceremony tenmoku bowls were used. These had of course crossed from China and, consequently, celadon and Tzü chou or pure white Chinese porcelain followed. Tea bowls of the Korean Koryo dynasty began to be used towards the end of the 16th century. It is said that Ido bowls of the Koryo were ranked as suitable for court use. The versions of the Ido type fired in southern Korea from the end of Koryo to the beginning of the Yi dynasty are considered best. They are shallow with a morning glory flower shape and a grey loquat glaze. Apart from one Ido tea bowl, there is a noodle bowl called after the Bear River in Korea (Komogae). All these bowls, even including the Ido bowl, had their origin in vessels used for everyday purposes. It was the tea men of old who discovered their beauty among such ordinary vessels.

36

There are various shapes of tea bowls, which are generally distinguished into those for use with the portable brazier and an ordinary brazier; in other words, winter-use and summer-use vessels. The former employ a shallow lip and the latter a deep lip. Furthermore, different bowls are used in making thick or thin powdered tea. In making thick powdered tea, somewhat large bowls of the Koryo type or the undecorated Raku type are used. For thin powdered tea a painted enamel bowl such as that originated by Ninsei and Kenzan is used. Apart from these, the tea bowls fired in Japan are Hagi, Asahi, Akahada, Seto, Ko-sobe, Oribe, Shino, Izumo, Karatsu et cetera. Of these Hagi and Oribe may be used in making thin tea. There are as well many hand-made bowls fired from clay pinched out by tea men themselves.

Hagi is a pot fired in the Hagi region of Yamaguchi Prefecture. It began with the forced immigration to Japan of the Korean potter, Ri-kei, who later changed his name to Korai Saemon. Hagi pots are tea vessels with a turbid glaze, the tea bowls of which have an especially high reputation.

Nonomura Ninsei was an early Edo potter who took his name from the village he came from, Tanba Nonomura. The character Nin in his other title, Ninsei, was bestowed by the Abbot of Omuro Ninna-ji Temple, an imperial prince. Ninsei made everything from small vessels like incense containers to large things like tea jars, but his speciality was enamel decoration on ceramics in the manner of lacquer inlay.

Mishima is a Korean-style ware on the inner and outer surface of which there is an incised rope-pattern decoration. This design was called Mishima because it resembled the design of the calendrical signs published by Mishima Shrine in Shizuoka Prefecture.

Mishima   Ninsei (Fan pattern)   Hagi

It was also imitated in Japan at Karatsu, Yatsushiro, and Tsushima. Apart from the tea bowls, there are also Mishima water jars.

Shino was fired in the Mino region. It has simple underglaze iron designs painted beneath a thickly applied and semitransparent white feldspar glaze.

Raku ware began with Rikyu, and is the most suitable tea bowl ware for use in the tea ceremony.

1. Shino
2. Red raku
3. Black raku

2

3

39

Round kettle (Marugama)   The 'evergreen' kettle

Iron tea kettles

Rikyu said in a poem that the most important thing needed to make tea is a kettle. The history of kettles begins when the monk Myoe of Kozan-ji Temple had a kettle made by a kettle master in Ashiya, Ongagun, in the then Chikuzen province of Kyushu. Onto it the words 'the ten virtues of tea' were moulded. However, whilst this kettle was made at the end of the Kamakura period, the actual demand for kettles comes after the succeeding Muromachi period when the kettles used in the tea ceremony were made in various parts of the country.

There are various names and shapes for kettles. There are kettles with patterns on their bulging portion, 'hailstone' kettles with a lumpy surface texture, kettles which are hung in the mouth of a portable brazier, and a kettle called 'Cloud

Dragon' which has a narrow cylindrical shape. Kettles are roughly distinguished into the large-sized ones used with an ordinary brazier and the small-sized ones used with a portable brazier. The ear of kettles are on both sides and vary according to whose preference the particular kettle had been, but the representative ones are· devil's mask ears and jasmine flower ears.

The oldest kettle shape is the shinnari or standard kettle. These were kettles usually made for use with a portable brazier.

Cicada-
braid kettle

However, large-sized ones may also be hung on an ordinary brazier.

An ordinary brazier is made from a brazier stand inserted into a section cut out of the alcove boards. It has a wooden frame 42cms square inside which the four walls are coated with plaster. A burner is put in the middle and a kettle hung on the tripod placed over it. In order to make the brazier more aesthetically pleasing, a skirting board is inserted around it. For this plain mulberry, chestnut, or Japan cedar wood is used when the room is a small one. In a tea room of larger than four and a half mats, a skirting board of lacquer or beautiful lacquer inlay is inserted. Such braziers began at about the time of Takeno Jo-o.

Brazier with a standard kettle (Shinnari)

Portable brazier with a kettle

Iron brazier

Portable brazier

These were first made of Chinese bronze for use with the tea stand. But from the time of Jo-o, portable braziers made of clay were used. These are called 'clay braziers' of which there are various shapes. The clay is fired and the top coated with black lacquer which is then polished. There are also braziers made of iron which imitate the shape of the clay brazier. A board is laid out beneath the clay brazier called the 'bedding board'. When an iron brazier is used, a tile is laid out called the 'bedding tile'.

Tea whisks

The whisk employed during the Sung dynasty in China was like a bamboo spatula whose tip had been finely divided. It was remade in various ways after it came to Japan. The shape of the present tea whisk comes from about the Muromachi period. It is said to have begun when Murata Shuko had one made by someone called Takayama Sosetsu. There are many kinds of tea whisks. However, the rough-headed whisk and the fine-headed whisk varieties may be generally distinguished. The latter whisk is used with thin powdered tea because of the many thin ends. The former has a rough head and is used with thick powdered tea. Since thick powdered tea differs from the thin variety in that the powdered tea has been polished, the stronger head is better. It is one of the tea man's precepts that the tea whisk is changed on each occasion guests are welcomed.

left:
Rough head
(Araho)

right:
Fine head
(Kazuho)

Cake utensils

The formal procedure in the tea room is for guests to be offered cakes served on a high-sided lacquer dish. These were once not just today's delicacies, but, because they were part of the formal tea ceremony meal, included fruit and boiled items as well. In recent times cakes have been separated from the formal meal. When with the coming of sugar, various new things were made, they were served on a cake dish rather than the high-sided lacquer dish as previously. Those cakes served on a cake dish are called 'wet' cakes (Omogashi) and those called 'dry cakes' (Higashi) of the rice biscuit or rice jelly variety are served on a tray.

'Wet cakes' are used with thick tea, and 'dry cakes' with thin tea.

Oribe dish

◀ Glassware

▼ Cake bowls

Bizen   Curved plain wood

Waste water containers

These are vessels for disposing of the water which was used to wash the tea bowl. On formal occasions they are made of plain curved wood. In the simple and natural tea ceremony, the lid of a southern water jar or a folk art hip lunch box is used as a waste water container. Even amongst the ceramic vessels there are many kinds of waste water vessels which are fired according to region, which variously include Bizen and Iga wares. There are also vessels made of Chinese bronze, and shapes such as long and thin, and flat and shallow, which are used after consideration of their suitability to the other utensils.

When the container is of plain wood a new one is used each time guests are welcomed. This is so that its unclean task of disposing of the water in which the bowl was washed may not be revealed to the guests. The use of a new vessel is therefore one of the courtesies of the tea man.

Lid rest

At first the gold rest for an ink stick was used as the lid rest in China. But Rikyu then made a lid rest of bamboo and there were so many different shapes made later of ceramic, iron, or Chinese bronze that they are now uncountable.

In the past lid rests were quietly hidden in the waste-water container and, if they were taken out, were put in some unprominent position. After that they began to be placed somewhere which reached the guests' attention, such as being displayed on a shelf or by the brazier when making tea. At the end of tea preparation when a shelf was used, the lid rest is displayed on the shelf together with the tea scoop. However, a bamboo lid rest is displayed by itself.

Various lid rests

Flower containers

Flowers are arranged in the alcove to add something to the brilliance of the tea room. A flower container is necessary for this and in the way of tea containers of old copper, celadon and pottery, bamboo, basket ware and so forth and used as befits the occasion.

▲ Hanging flower container

◀ Hanging scroll and bamboo flower container

Old Copper   Southern   Basket
Barbarian
style

A nail is fixed in the centre of the tea room wall from which a flower container is hung. Flowers are also arranged in a flower vase hung on the nail from which the hanging scroll has been removed. A single camelia is tasteful when arranged in a bamboo flower container or a pinch pot of Shiga-raki or Ohi ware. Bamboo flower containers exist from the time of Jōō, but the usual theory is that they begin with one cut by Rikyu on Mt. Nira at Hideyoshi's behest, on the occasion of the conquest of Odawara. Flower containers of Chinese bronze came from China as Buddhist utensils, and their name varies according to the shape.

The flower container is selected according to the rank of the hanging scroll in the alcove.

Bronze ▶
flower
container

left: for use with a portable brazier
right: for use with an ordinary brazier

Incense containers

It is the taste of tea people to burn incense before the guests enter the tea room. The charcoal fire must be prepared before tea is made, and the charcoal replenished in the brazier. When this is accomplished, the fire is stoked with incense. In the portable brazier season wood incense like aloes or sandal wood is used with a container of lacquer or lacquer inlay. With an ordinary brazier a pastille compressed from various kinds of incense is used such as 'plum incense'. Here the container used is ceramic. When there are many guests and it is impossible to prepare the charcoal and incense beforehand for each guest individually, the incense container is displayed in the alcove on a napkin or a paper kettle mat.

The preparation room for utensils.
This is always kept in good order.

THE PRECEPTS OF THE GUESTS

The guest first considers the purpose of the tea ceremony when the invitation is received. For example, the guest considers whether the ceremony is a celebration, whether it is just a gathering of friends to enjoy tea, or whether it is a formal occasion to be followed by a meal. The next thing a guest examines is whether there is any notification of who the other guests are, whether some special person will be participating, whether the number of guests is restricted and, if the number is undecided, between what times the guests should arrive. After considering such matters, a reply confirming presence or absence is sent as soon as possible.

The inviting party too should write something on the notification card about the purpose of the tea ceremony. I think it is kind to at least add something like 'The other guests are so and so, with whom you are well acquainted'.

If the tea ceremony is to be informal and unstrained with only thin tea to be served, ordinary clothes will be satisfactory, and, depending on the occasion, there will be no objection to Western clothes. It is desirable that the guests should aim to arrive between twenty and thirty minutes earlier than the specified time. On arriving early, socks are changed in the hall and the completion of the number of other guests is awaited in the preparation room. When their number is made up, the guests set out on the roji under the guidance of the host.

When the guests are settled down on the bench in the waiting arbour (1), the host comes out to welcome them and opens the middle gate. The guests rise together and they and the host make a wordless bow. (2) Waiting for the host to retire, the guests proceed to the stone water-basin beginning with the

56

1

2

57

3

principle guest. She first fills the ladle with water and washes both hands. (3) Next she rinses her mouth (4), and, holding the ladle up, washes its handle. (5) She then returns the ladle to the basin. One ladle of water is used without any wastage.

4

5

6

7

The guest mounts the stone in front of the crawling entrance, on which shoes are removed, and quietly opens the door. After once looking into the tea room, the guest grasps the door will with both hands and goes up, as if crawling, with the head lowered. (6) Tea men of old instruct that the guest dispels worldly thoughts and becomes detached at the moment the entrance is gone under. But even without thinking so deeply, the crawling entrance may be considered a place which composes the guest's feelings. On entering, the guest turns back to the entrance, and, taking her own sandals, stands them back to back against the wall by the stone. (7) There are people who think it is contradictory to handle sandals just after having washed one's hands, but I think the washing of hands is, above all, for cleansing the heart.

The principal guest first proceeds to the alcove

on entering the tea room and, after lightly bowing, with her fan by her knee, the guest views the hanging scroll. (8) Above all, the guest looks at the words written on the scroll and carefully confirms whether it is an old calligraph, a one-line poem, or a poetry fragment. The hanging scroll is rather like the title of that day's tea ceremony. The other utensils used in the ceremony are harmonised with the words on the hanging scroll, and the guest understands from them whether today's ceremony is a celebration or a festival. The guest looks at the words, the mounting of the scroll, and so forth. Next the body is turned to face the flower container which is viewed and the flower examined. The flower container may be placed on the floor or hung up from a column of the alcove. The flower was, moreover, selected with great effort by the host, so it is examined carefully.

8

9

10

When viewing of the alcove is completed, utensils on the rice mat are viewed, such as the brazier, the kettle, and the shelf of the tea stand. (9) For this the guest sits in a way which will not inconvenience the others. Like the principal guest, the other guests also view the alcove, the brazier, the kettle, and the shelf of the tea stand. When this is all completed they sit in allotted places and await the host. (10) First cakes are brought to the guests. (11)

It is formal etiquette to set the wet sweets out before each guest in a lacquer cake dish. The guests put out a paper napkin in front of their knees and take a cake onto the napkin with the wooden pick, which is arranged on the cake dish. (12) The cake is then cut up with the pick into easily digestible pieces and is eaten.

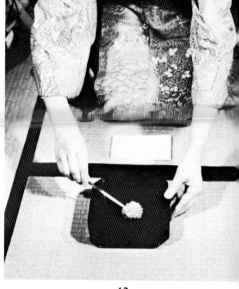

12

The lacquer cake dishes are in a set of about five to which a lid is added. Just enough wooden picks are arranged on the lid for the number of guests, each of whom takes a pick from the lid at the same time as removing the lowest dish. The remaining dishes are handed on to the next guest.

If the lacquer cake dish is omitted, wet cakes just sufficient for the number of guests are served on a cake dish completed by a pair of wooden chopsticks.

Dry cakes are served on a plate in about two varieties. For example, coloured rice-jelly cakes pressed into a shape

13

are often served. Since the guests may take two kinds of dry cake, the dish is served with a surplus of two or three portions. After the guest has lightly bowed to the host in accepting the cake dish, she brings out a paper napkin and takes a cake with chopsticks. (13) She wipes the tip of the chopsticks with the edge of the paper, and puts them on top of the cake dish which she passes to the next guest. When guests want to examine the cake dish, they put the chopsticks on the paper napkin, pick up the dish in their hands, and examine it, then replace the chopsticks on the dish.

14

As the next guest takes a wet cake, the principal guest takes the dry cake dish in front of her. After complimenting the host with the words 'I gratefully accept these things', she lightly grasps the dish and takes a cake with her fingers. (14) If two kinds of cake are served, they are taken from the side nearest her and put on the paper napkin with the wet cake. It is acceptable to take the plate in both hands when examining it, but the guest is careful not to disarrange the cakes served on it.

It is acceptable to eat the cake when the dish has been passed to the next guest. The guest takes the paper with the cake on it into her hand. But when a lacquer cake dish is used, the cake is eaten after division by the wooden pick into easily digestible portions. (15)

It is better to finish eating the cake before the tea bowl is put out, but, should there be anything left uneaten, this may be nimbly wrapped in the paper napkin and put on one side of the knee. Such cake may be taken home and eaten later.

15

THE ETIQUETTE OF TEA PREPARATION

Training in the etiquette of tea preparation begins with the basic etiquette, in the perfection or imperfection of which the quality of a tea ceremony is decided. In the basic etiquette the polishing of the lacquer caddy, the cleaning of the tea whisk and the wiping of the tea bowl are trained. The tea ceremony is finely divided into details such as folding the napkin and wiping the scoop and so forth, but its etiquette is the overall sum of these details.

The etiquette of tea is broadly distinguished into that for making thin powdered tea and that for thick powdered tea, which vary according to whether a portable or an ordinary brazier is used. There is a further etiquette for making tea using a shelf. These, then, are the bases of tea etiquette which, whilst remaining generally the same, slightly varies according to the utensils employed.

In addition to the etiquette of making tea, there is also an etiquette in the preparation of the charcoal fire. Before tea is made, the fire is fed with fuel. The fire is replenished during the making of thick and thin tea in a way which also differs according to the brazier employed.

There are schools of tea whose etiquette varies for men and women. However, in the three Senke schools it seems there is scarcely any difference. Where tea is prepared by a woman, her clothes should be of solid colour where possible. A man's clothes are of solid colour. It is formal etiquette for him to wear clothes called the 'Ten virtues', which are one variation of the clothes of a priest. (16) They are of black linen or gauze and hang as far as the hips. The 'Ten virtues' are generally worn in schools of the Senke line. But in schools of the Daimyo (Great lords) line, such as the Enshu and Sekishu

16

schools, the 'Ten virtues' are not worn and tea is prepared wearing a man's formal pleated skirt. However, these days young people are preparing tea, and many of them and their guests do so wearing Western clothes.

Let us now return to the tea room.

The host prepares tea whilst the guests are eating the cakes. (17) The right quantity of tea to put in the bowl is about one full scoop and a half, for which the appropriate amount of hot water is about three and a half mouthfuls.

17 If too much water is added a froth will be difficult to work up and the taste will be unpleasant as well. In contrast, if the quantity of water is insufficient, the tea will be difficult to drink. Tea is not made by whisking round and round but in a to and fro movement from the shoulder, not just the wrist. When tea is made and put out in the tea bowl, the principal guest comes out to fetch it. (18) The principal guest first puts the bowl inside the edge of the rice mat between herself and the next guest, and greets her with the words 'Excuse me for drinking before you'. (19) The guest places the tea bowl inside the edge of the mat in front of her knee. After greeting the host with the words 'I gratefully accept the tea you have prepared', the guest lifts the

18

bowl with her
right hand resting
it in the palm of
her left, and then
bows lightly.

19

If this is done with felicity the guest thereby expresses her gratitude in accepting a bowl of tea. I think this idea certainly originated in Buddhist thought, but even were it not the case, the feeling of gratitude shown by the guest is her courtesy in response to the host's efforts to prepare just one cup of tea. Greeting the guests and putting out a kettle is a lot of work for the host, whose energy will be both physically and spiritually consumed in sweeping the rōji and preparing the tea room. The front of the tea bowl faces the guest which she turns so that the opposite side is now nearest her. This is to avoid having the front of the bowl face the guest when drinking from it. (20) The guest wipes the part of the rim she has drunk from with her finger tip, (21) and then wipes her finger on the paper napkin. The tea bowl is turned back and placed outside the edge of the rice mat with the front facing the guest. She examines the total shape, (22) and with both hands underneath lifts it up and

20

21

examines details of the bowl. The bowl is safely held if both elbows are rested on the knees and a low posture maintained. (23) The principal guest puts the bowl outside the edge of the mat again and re-examines it before placing it inside the edge between herself and the next guest. The principal guest says 'Excuse me for drinking before you'.

When preparation of tea is completed, the guests view the lacquer caddy and the tea scoop. On being greeted by the guests, the host puts these utensils out for them. (24)

After placing the utencils by her right knee, the principal guest begins viewing with the lacquer caddy. This is placed outside the edge of the rice mat and examined overall. The lid is then opened and the body of the caddy examined by hand. The tea scoop is viewed next.

22　　　　　**23**

24

The lacquer caddy still has tea left in it which may be spilt on the rice mat if the guest is not attentive. The tea scoop should not be held above the joint. When all the guests have completed viewing the utensils the principal guest returns them to the place at which they were first put out. The host comes out to get them, at which point the principal guest enquires 'What kind of shape has this caddy?', to which the host replies, 'It is a medium caddy'. The principal guest then asks various questions about the objects, such as 'Who was the lacquer inlay craftsman?', 'Which tea masters liked this caddy?', 'Whose work is the tea scoop?', 'Has it any special name?'.

25

After replying to these questions, the host withdraws the tea caddy and scoop. She sits outside the door to the way of tea and makes a single bow to the guests. (25) They too reply with a single bow. This ends the tea ceremony, and those guests who are unfamiliar with it should come out into the middle of the tea room to see and remember the appearance of the other people who are guests.

The utensils used in the shortened etiquette on a tray

THE SHORTENED ETIQUETTE, USING
A PORTABLE BRAZIER

This is the simplest way of preparing tea. It may be carried out in places aside from the tea room. The necessary utensils are an iron kettle or an ordinary kitchen kettle and a small-type brazier. If there is not one of these, the kettle may be rested on a tea pot mat. The shortened etiquette should be possible with only the following utensils: – a round tray about 30 cms in diameter, a tea bowl, a lacquer caddy, a tea scoop and a whisk, a tea cloth and a waste water container – in place of which any handy bowl will suffice. If there is no lacquer caddy, the tea canister may be used as it stands, or, with a little extra work, coloured paper may be stuck to the canister and a relatively attractive caddy be produced.

The caddy is put on the tray on the side away from the host and the tea bowl of the side nearest her. The host makes a single bow with the tray level by her right knee and the napkin tucked in by her hip. (1) The host comes into the tea room carrying the tray which she sets up in front of the kettle and brazier. (2) The host next brings out the waste water container in her left hand and, sitting with the tray in front of her, puts the container by her left knee. (3) At this point the host takes the napkin at her hip into her left hand and folds it. (4) The method of folding varies with the school of tea, nevertheless it must be practiced fully as basic training. The napkin is folded in order to wipe the lacquer caddy and tea scoop, but the action of wiping actually serves to purify the spirit. The host wipes the lacquer caddy and the scoop in the preparation room beforehand, consequently these are clean when brought out on the tray. They are wiped in front of the guests so that what is clean may also be purified. (5) (6)

1

4

6

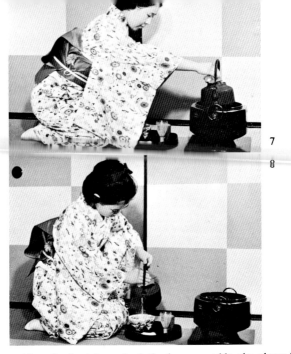

After the host has wiped the lacquer caddy she places it a little to the left of its original position. The tea scoop is lent against the right edge of the tray after wiping.

The host puts out the tea whisk to the right of the caddy and puts the tea cloth by the end of the tea scoop. She shifts the napkin to her right hand and shuts the lid of the kettle. (7) The host then lifts the kettle by the handle and, holding the lid with the napkin, fills the tea bowl with hot water. (8) She returns the kettle and hangs the napkin over the left edge of the tray.

The host lifts the tea whisk and cleans it. With the tip of the

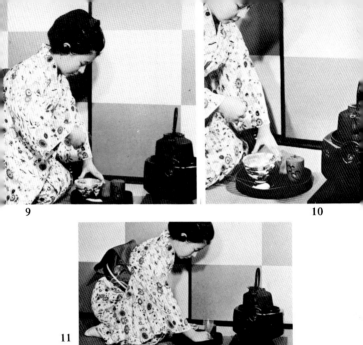

9

10

11

whisk in the tea bowl of hot water, she first lightly knocks the
handle of the whisk against the edge of the bowl, then lifts the
whisk out (9) and knocks the handle against the side again.
After re-inserting the head of the whisk, she lifts it out again (10)
and knocks the handle against the side for the third time. Then
after the host has smoothly rinsed the tea whisk round the bowl,
it is returned to its original position. (11) The host then lifts
the tea bowl in her right hand and disposes of the hot water
with her left. (12) At the same time as disposing of the water,
the host takes the tea cloth in her right hand (13) and,
opening it out one fold, hangs it on the edge of the tea bowl. (14)

12

13   14

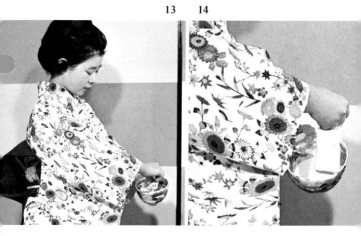

15

16

This she wipes by rotating it three and a half times. She then puts the tea cloth inside the bowl and wipes it four times. With her right hand she puts the bowl on the tray, just as it is with the cloth in it. The host then takes the cloth out with her right hand and returns it to its original position.

The tea cloth is made of white linen or bleached Nara cotton. After soaking with water in the preparation room, it is wrung well and put in the tea bowl folded. If it is used when dry, the tea bowl will be difficult to wipe.

When the tea cloth is returned to its original position, the host lifts the tea scoop in her right hand, at the same time greeting the guests with the words 'Please take a cake'. (15) The host withdraws the hand holding the scoop to her right knee and, on lifting the caddy with her left hand, removes the lid with her right, which still grips the tea scoop. The host stands the lid up at the edge of the tray where the scoop was earlier.

17

The host fills the scoop with tea which she puts into the bowl. (16) She lightly knocks the scoop against the edge of the bowl so that the tea which adheres to the end falls off. The host replaces the lid of the caddy and returns it to its original position. She rests the tea scoop on the edge of the tray where it had been earlier. The host takes the napkin with her right hand, the tea kettle with her left, and fills the tea bowl with hot water. The napkin and kettle are then returned to their places. She then takes hold of the whisk and prepares tea. When it is made the host takes the bowl with her right hand, resting the bowl on the palm of her left, (17) turns it so that the front faces the guest, to whom she then gives it. (18) (19) The guest's etiquette is no different from that of the usual tea ceremony, but they should not adhere to too much formality.

When the bowl is returned the host lifts it with her right hand and, assisted by her left, puts it on the tray. She then takes the napkin, lifts the kettle and fills the tea bowl with

18

19

20

21   22

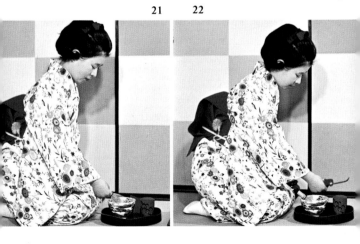

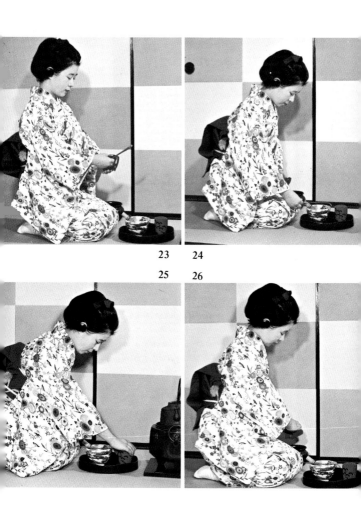

23　24

25　26

87

27

hot water. She disposes of the water after washing the bowl, which she then wipes with the tea cloth.

Anyone can learn how to make tea if they repeat this procedure many times.

Once tea has been extended to each guest alike, the principal guest greets the host with the words 'Please bring the ceremony to a close' just as the host rinses the tea bowl and disposes of the water with the waste water container. The host, who has the tea bowl in her left hand, asks 'Would you like some hot water?'. (20) If the principal guest replies 'We have sufficient', the host makes the greeting 'I will now bring the ceremony to a close'. She takes the napkin, lifts the kettle, and fills the tea bowl with hot water. The host then returns the napkin and kettle to their places, takes the tea whisk and cleans it.

The host washes the head of the whisk first and then taps it against the side of the bowl. She withdraws the whisk, taps it once more, and then returns it to the original position on the tray. She next disposes of the hot water, puts the tea cloth inside on the bottom of the bowl and the whisk on top of it. (21) The host takes the tea scoop with her right hand (22) and pulls the water container back a little with her left hand.

28   29

The host then refolds the napkin with the hand holding the scoop and, after wiping the scoop a second time, (23) rests it on the bowl. (24) She next pushes the caddy aside a little to the right (25) and rinses out the tea which has adhered to the napkin. (26) She tucks the napkin back in her waist after opening the lid of the kettle slightly. (27) (28)

The host now pulls back the water container on her own side (29) and, after moving out to get the tray, withdraws it with both hands to her own side, placing it level with her knee. The host then makes a single bow.

The above is the shortened etiquette, which, as I said in the beginning, may be carried out anywhere at all. If a tea bowl and caddy are always kept in readiness in a corner of a room, should there be a guest, tea may be prepared by just bringing a kettle and waste water container from the kitchen.

The practice of the tea ceremony is not only to acquire skill in polite manners inside and outside the tea room. It seems to be not entirely useless in the creation of such manners in everyday social life.

Moreover, the way of tea does not only teach deportment in everyday life. For we may ask what sort of frame of mind if necessary in exchanges between people. In what way do we accept the solicitudes of other people? This is what is learnt in the way of tea. Besides, a heart which seeks beauty is cultivated through an appreciation of the utensils employed and from the economy of physical deportment learnt through the etiquette.

THE MEAL SERVED DURING
THE FORMAL TEA CEREMONY

The word for this meal, kaiseki, originated in the Zen sect.
It is the name for the heated stones placed in the pocket over
the stomach when the monks were meditating during a fast. The
gastric juices were stimulated and they were able to relieve
their hunger. Consequently, the simple meal in the way of tea
which just tides over hunger is called kaiseki.

A rice bowl is laid on the left and soup bowl on the right
of a small tray. A small dish of fish salad or raw sliced fish
is served in front of it. Apart from these dishes, the cuisine
includes boiled and fried food, another soup at the end, after
which 'mountain and sea' food is offered on a square tray of
plain wood.

Eating the meal proceeds by first simultaneously removing
the lids from the rice and soup bowls. These are placed level
with the right side of the tray. The rice bowl is filled with
enough rice for one or two mouthfuls, as is the soup bowl.
When eating is completed and the lids replaced, the host puts
out just enough sake cups for the number of guests on cup rests
and brings them out with the sake bottle. The guests drink sake
together from these cups. Sake is rarely drunk at the same time
as the food above. The rice container is next put out from
which guests serve themselves into their rice bowls. The host
offers more soup and then carries in the boiled and fried food.
The latter is taken onto the vessel opposite the guest on the
tray. Soup and 'mountain and sea' food are served in succession.
At the same time the principal guest refills the sake cups and
when this is completed, pickles and hot water are served. The

hot water is poured over the small amount of rice left aside by the guest, which is now eaten with the hot water.

It seems easy to write about the food service in this way since there are also rules of decorum for eating kaiseki. Among such rules which have been laid down are those of not making a noise when drinking soup, that the lips must not be smacked, and that it is bad manners to leave food in the bowl. These are the Zen rules of decorum when eating which were adopted by the way of tea as they stand.

a rice ▶
container

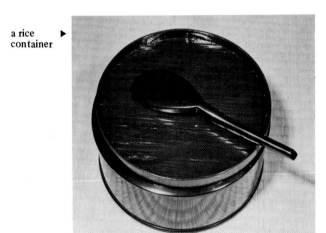

Simple tea ceremony food service

The complete tea ceremony food service
left: Rice bowl   right: Soup bowl

95

Juko-in, sub-temple of the Daitoku-ji Temple

'An Introduction to the Tea Ceremony' was written for people who wanted to know about the way of tea and to begin practicing the tea ceremony. I have therefore written about how the way of tea was established, about the roji and the tea room and about the etiquette of the ceremony because I wanted to avoid prejudice towards a particular school.

The Way of Tea is now receiving worldwide attention. I think that as Japanese we need to re-examine the Way of Tea whether or not we are learning it. We might first here proceed under the gate of Juko-in, the temple of Rikyu, the Buddhist layman. This is surely the gate which leads to the Way of Tea.

Ido tea bowl

I. THE HISTORY OF THE WAY OF TEA

The crossing of tea from China

It goes without saying that China is the original home of the habit of tea drinking. In the T'ang dynasty (618–907) of China, tea drinking had already flourished to the extent that a book called the Tea Sutra was published. It was written by the T'ang man of letters, Lu Yu, in 760, and discusses the history of tea in China, its method of manufacture, utensils, the method of preparation, and the way tea is drunk.

The word 'brick tea' is written in the Sutra. This is tea whose leaves are steamed, put in a tea mill and pounded, and are then compressed into a round brick. The right amount of tea is shaved off the brick and hot water is poured on to the shavings. It is the resulting liquor which is drunk. Tea in this form is easy to carry and can also be preserved for a long time. It seems that brick tea is still used in the interior of China.

There are no accurate materials which survive to tell us when tea was first imported from China. But we may surmise that tea was imported in the Nara period through Buddhist priests coming from China and India and through the Japanese envoys who crossed to T'ang China.

The first Japanese Tea Plantation

The monk Saicho went to China in 802 and returned some years later bringing with him the seeds of the tea plant. These he planted in Sakamoto at the foot of the holy mountain of Hieizan he had inaugurated, and on which he built Enryaku-ji Temple.

The tea plant takes about five years for the seeds to be sown, the buds to sprout and the bush to be cultivated before tea leaves may be picked. By 815 the tea plants Saicho had planted at Sakamoto had grown splendidly.

In June of that year the Emperor Saga visited Karasaki in the province of Omi and called in on the way at the Sufuku-ji Temple. It is said that on this occasion the abbot of Sufuku-ji, Eichu, offered the Emperor tea he had infused himself. Eichu went to T'ang China at the end of the Nara period and returned in attendance on the Japanese envoy at the beginning of the Heian period. It therefore seems probable he learnt the method of tea production and tea drinking. The tea he offered the Emperor Saga was probably infused from leaves picked at Sakamoto which he had refined himself. It moreover appears that this was not the brick tea hitherto employed, but was a tea hardly different to green tea (sencha), which, like today, was drunk from hot water poured on to tea leaves.

The tea plantation in Sakamoto still remains as the oldest in Japan. Tea production increased because the Emperor, who had learnt the flavour from Eichu, encouraged the making of tea plantations in the various provinces hear the imperial palace. The habit of tea drinking then widened among the monks and nobility — that is among the aristocratic class.

The contemporary manner of tea drinking closely resembled that for making brick tea, but, in the case of this sencha-like tea, the leaves were first dried and ground into a powder on a handmill, they were then hardened by kneading and dried again. It was stored in the form of brick tea which was flaked off as necessary, boiled and drunk with sweetners like sweet arrowroot, and aromatics like ginger.

Poems were written and recited whilst drinking tea, since the period was one of the imitation of Chinese culture among aristocrats, monks and literati. The Chinese style of tea drinking spread in this way up to the beginning of the Heian period. But when the dispatch of envoys to China was abrogated in 894, the light of Chinese learning was gradually extinguished. In its place there was a sudden rise in Japanese literature which had not been worthy of attention since the Manyoshu poetry anthology. The custom of drinking tea, which had been connected to Chinese learning, died out as well.

The crossing of powdered tea from China

When the Heike clan became powerful at the end of the Heian period, diplomatic relations were revived after an interval of 280 years with the contemporary Sung China. The number of monks going to China increased with the re-opening of communications and the first of these was the Zen priest Eisai, who returned home in 1191. On landing at Hirado in Kyushu, he planted the tea seed he had brought back from China in the front garden of the Iwagami Lodge of the Reisen-ji Temple at Seburi-yama in the province of Hizen. The remains of this garden survive even today, but what is more important than Eisai's having brought back tea seeds from China is the fact that he also transmitted Rinzai Zen Buddhism to Japan. The Zen sect was begun by Bodhi dharma in China in about the sixth century, and had been transmitted to Japan by Eichu in the early Heian period, but had died out after him. It was Eisai who re-transmitted Zen in the thirteenth century.

In 1202, when Eisai came to Kyoto to open the Kennin-ji Temple on the order of the second Heike military dictator, Yoriie, he put five tea seeds in a pottery vessel the shape of a persimmon and gave them to Myoe Shonin of Toganoo Kozan-ji Temple. The tea seeds test cultivated at Toganoo bore fruit and so the tea was once again transplanted, on this occasion to Yamashiro at Uji, where it became the basis for the current prosperity of Uji tea. This tea was in its turn further transplanted to other areas and tea plantations scattered throughout the whole country and the production of green tea therefore increased. By this time, however, powdered tea (matcha) was already in use in China.

Matcha is tea made into a powder by grinding leaves in a tea mill, and is different from the brick tea of the T'ang dynasty and the aromatic green tea (sencha) of the Ming dynasty. Not only is the liquor drunk which was infused from the refined leaves, but, since the powdered tea has completely diffused into the liquor, all the tea is drunk and there are therefore many additional nutritive benefits. Eisai learnt how to drink and prepare powdered tea during his stay in China.

Kissa-yojo-ki (notes on the curative effects of tea)

Eisai carried on writing about the virtues of powdered tea as ordinarily used in China in a two-volume treatise he authored called 'Kissa-yojo-ki' (Notes on the curative effects of tea). Eisai writes in this book that the health of the five human organs is strengthened through the plentiful intake of the five flavours they each respectively enjoy. Accordingly, the lung enjoys sharp flavours, the liver desires sour flavours, the spleen sweet flavours, the kidney salty flavours and the heart enjoys bitter flavours. But, whilst people absorb the four flavours of sharp, sour, sweet and salty, the bitter flavour necessary for the heart is unpleasant and cannot be taken in. This is the reason, Eisai writes, why Japanese hearts are afflicted and Japanese lives short. We are fortunately able to learn from the people of the continent and we must make our hearts healthy by absorbing the bitter flavour of tea. He interprets tea drinking as a secret technique for the prolongation of life. The drinking of tea gradually spread thereafter because Eisai's purpose in writing 'Kissa-yojo-ki' was to use tea drinking as one method of meritorious religious practice.

In addition he wrote in 'Kissa-yojo-ki' about the way of drinking powdered tea. According to this treatise two or three scoopfuls of powdered tea are put in a tea bowl and boiling water is poured on to them. The mixture is then churned up with a whisk and drunk.

This was the era of the third Kamakura military dictator, Sanetomo, who, when he was ill from heavy drinking, had summoned Eisai and had commanded him to make spells and incantations. Eisai had presented him with 'Kissa-yojo-ki' and some powdered tea, saying it was an even better medicine than spells. Sanetomo was pleased with the recuperation he made from his illness and even recommended the drinking of powdered tea to his trusted vassals.

The drinking of powdered tea in the Kamakura period

Myoe Shonin was famous as an eminent monk who had revived the Kegon (Avatamska) sect, one of the sects of Nara Buddhism. He not only received tea from Eisai, but also learnt Zen and tea etiquette with him. Myoe thought that there were three poisons in the practice of Zen discipline. One was sleepiness, one was idle thoughts, and one was an improper meditation posture. If these three poisons could not be eliminated he thought it would be difficult to attain merit, even if the days and months were spent exerting heart and body. Drowsiness was a particular impediment to Zen meditational austerities for the elimination of which only the drinking of powdered tea would suffice. This was encouraged among monks as a contribution to their religious practices through the emphasis put on tea by Myoe Shonin. The etiquette of preparing powdered tea spread not only among the Zen sect but also to the Kegon sect and the Ritsu (Laws) sect.

The Priest Eison, who had restored the fortunes of Saidai-ji Temple at Nara, came down to Kamakura in 1262 on the invitation of Hojo Sanetomo. On the way he carried out the Buddhist confirmation ceremony for those who requested it, and gave powdered tea to the assembled crowds, probably as a medicine of longevity. Moreover, just as he paid homage inside the precincts of Saidai-ji to the tutelary god Hachiman, snow fell very hard. He considered this to be an auspicious omen and made a tea offering in the shrine. The tea left over was infused in a large vessel and bestowed on the assembled populace. This was the origin of the Great Tea-Offering Ceremony at Saidai-ji which has taken place down to the present day on the 15th and 16th of April every year.

The tea drinking of the Kamakura period therefore began through the monks who first offered tea to Buddha, and then the remainder was drunk by the participating monks and populace. This custom was ceremonialised by the Monk Dogen, who had transmitted Sodo Zen. Dogen was taught by Eisai, and had crossed to Southern Sung China where he had meditated. He had learnt the 'Pure Rules of Pai chang' which had been laid down by the famous Chinese monk, Pai chang. Dogen had included a selection from these rules in his 'Rules for Eihei-ji Temple', and had laid down the offering of tea as a part of daily Zen religious exercise. These rules brought about not just the drinking of powdered tea, but also something like an etiquette for drinking it.

The tea tournaments of the Northern and Southern Dynasties

The drinking of powdered tea by itself died out in China, but its drinking did become part of the tea tournament (tocha), which was merely a kind of licensed game. The powdered tea was drunk from the early Kamakura period by temple monks and those warriors who had become confirmed devotees of Buddhism, become instantly popular with the crossing of this game at the end of the Kamakura period. Its golden age was from the period of the Northern and Southern dynasties until the middle of the Muromachi period.

Tea tournaments were held in a two-storeyed building called a 'meeting place', the ground floor of which was called the guests' terrace and the upper, the tea drinking pavilion. The latter was a bright plank-floored room whose windows opened on all four sides to take in the view. There was no alcove; a screen was set up on the front side, and on it a set of three 'Chinese paintings' was hung. This consisted of an image of the Buddha in the centre, with buddhist pictures of Kannon (Avalokitesvara) and Seishibosatsu (Mahasthanaprapta) on both sides. A table was installed in front of the scroll ornamented with a flower vase, an incense container and a candlestick holder. These were called the 'three utensils' and were all of the 'Chinese things' variety. Desks were aligned in three corners of the room on which were placed a monk's light refreshments, cakes and gambling stakes. The monk's light refreshments consisted of simple food and the cakes were of rare fruits different to those of later times. The gambling stakes were a bonus to be received by the winner of the tournament.

The master of the tea tournament in the upper storey tea drinking pavilion was called the 'host'. It was customary for the guests to receive a banquet in the ground floor reception hall and, after dinner, to descend and saunter in the garden.

The layout of the garden changed because of this custom from the 'viewing' layout to the 'ambulatory' layout of the Ginkaku-ji Temple garden in Kyoto. Whilst the guests sauntered in the garden, the host made the preparations for the tea tournament and welcomed the guests in the tea drinking pavilion. The guests sat on a bench covered with leopardskin and the host sat in a bamboo chair set up on the floor. In due course a cup-bearer, who was frequently the child of the host, brought out three tea bowls and offered them before the Buddhist pictures at the front of the room. Tea bowls filled with powdered tea were next set out in front of the guests and the cup-bearer brought out a vase of boiling water and a tea whisk. The guests' tea bowls were filled with hot water which was mixed in with the tea whisk. When all the guests had drunk the first serving of powdered tea, new tea bowls were set out and tea offered. Different kinds of tea could be drunk and the 'right' and 'wrong' distinguished in this way, the 'right' tea having been picked at Toganoo and the 'wrong' tea having been picked in other areas of production. The gambling stakes were received according to the points won. Tea had therefore to be drunk many times and the tournaments were consequently named ten bowl, fifty bowl, and one hundred bowl tournaments.

Tea vessels of the 'Chinese things' variety were used as a rule incense containers and copper flower vases were displayed. The incensed containers and copper flower vases were displayed. The 'Chinese pictures' and so forth hung in the tea room gradually changed from Buddhist pictures to landscapes and to bird and flower pictures.

Street tea-pedlars ▶

The popularity of such tea tournaments presently diffused to wider society where they were called 'tea meetings'. But there were several abuses due to the gambling, to the extent that Takauji added a clause which absolutely forbade games whose purpose was gambling, to the feudal code he laid down in 1336. Yet the drinking of powdered tea gradually became more popular as a consequence of the increase in Japanese tea production. It began to be drunk in a simple fashion even by the class of ordinary citizens, and a new trade was created by people such as those selling tea outside temple gates, and those peddling it in the streets whose cries could be heard on street corners. The former constructed fixed shops which in later times became tea shops. However, the powdered tea drunk there was of course not the best, and even if a froth was worked up by the whisk, it soon disappeared. The froth 'sped away like clouds' and was therefore called 'moving clouds' (unkyaku).

The establishment of tea rites

In December 1361 Sasaki Doyo was attacked by the military forces of the Southern court and fled from the capital. He put out a set of tea utensils in a room of his own mansion, prepared food and drink, and even had his cup-bearers wait in readiness so that the generals of the attacking forces could hold a tea tournament right away. It is said that the way of displaying the utensils on that occasion, called 'Display in Seven places, for a Reception Room', became the basis on which the etiquette of tea was established.

However, the basis for the etiquette of tea was much older. In about the middle of the Kamakura period Ogasawara Sadamune had received lectures from Dogen on the 'Pure Rules of Pai chang' and had tried to establish rules of Zen temples. They were more or less completed by the Kitayama era of the early Muromachi period. Such rules of decorum were minutely regulated in the society of warrior households for the occasion of welcoming the arrival of guests and for the deportment when serving nobility. This was the origin of the Ogasawara etiquette and was consequently somewhat different to the Zen etiquette of tea because it had been established for warrior households. Yet the warriors' tea etiquette was still more or less a part of Zen etiquette.

An artist called Noami became 'companion' of the military dictator's household in the middle of the Muromachi period at the time of sixth military dictator, Yoshinori. The 'companion' was an artist who served as cultural advisor to the dictator. Noami laid down the 'Display of a tea stand for a Reception Room' using the 'Display in Seven Places for a Reception Room' as a reference. The tea stand is a shelf used in preparing tea which was formerly a utensil employed in the tea offering of Zen temples. (See P.19) It was displayed in the reception room and the tea offering of the warrior household was carried out with it.

It seems that the rules for the decoration of a reception room and the tea stand established by Noami were just about completed by the time of the era of Yoshimasa. At the same time the way of handling tea vessels and the code of measurements for harmonizing the relative sizes of utensils had been naturally arrived at.

The method of preparing tea, which has been transmitted down to the present day, was also conceived by Noami in consultation with the rules of decorum of the Ogasawara style. In addition the physical gestures used in the preparation of tea had taken up the steps of the dance in the Noh play, especially in the way of walking when moving utensils. There was no special dress for tea making, although in tea tournaments the host wore the old formal dress, monks wore a 'ten virtues' surplice, and the nobility wore a plain coat. Thus tea was made and people invited to it in the clothes of their rank or occupation.

The formation of the Way of Tea

A man called Murata Shuko (1433–1502) lived in Nara at the time of Yoshimasa. His precise biographical details are unknown apart from the fact that he liked tea from an early age. He amused himself in the tea tournaments of the Nara style then popular and he ran away from a temple because he had neglected his work. After wandering in various provinces, he finally entered the Shinju-an of Daitoku-ji Temple and underwent Zen training with the priest Ikkyu.

Shuko was enlightened during his austerities when it appeared to him that even the Law of Buddha may be discovered in the gestures of filling an ordinary tea bowl with hot water. That is he was enlightened not just in drinking tea but in trying to involve himself in the philosophy of the act of drinking tea. For example, a tea ceremony is offered every morning before

108

Buddha after which the tea is drunk. This ceremony is to pray that Buddha and the self may become one through drinking tea at the same time as offering it to Buddha.

This example apart, tea was also drunk together with others when something was discussed and decided. To drink tea with someone was also a pledge that an agreement would not be violated.

Shuko's tea was, apart from Buddhism, also flavoured with Confucianism. He put heavier emphasis on the problem of the heart of the person conducting and learning tea rather than the formalities of the tea rite. He taught 'Admonish egotism, be the teacher of your heart, do not let it be the teacher'. He also remonstrated against beginners being envious of the adept or of the adept despising the beginner.

The heart of a man of tea humbled in this way seeks to express itself naturally on the occasion of a tea ceremony in new ideas for tea meetings and in the appearance of tea ceremony. In explaining a simple and natural appearance Shuko thought that a 'refined idea' was to make tea using 'Chinese things' utensils of high value in a small room made of straw. The correct expression of this appearance was not something viewed from outside the hut, but was to be found in the solicitude of the host towards the guests.

Shuko later strung up a grass hut in the area of Sixth Precinct and Horikawa, and died in 1502 aged 81. He had wanted in the meantime to reform the tea ceremony towards the use of a rustic hut and a tea stand. When peace of mind could not be found in a large reception room, Shuko's ideal had been to cut a hole in the floor of a four and a half mat room, to enclose it with screens, to change the lacquer tea stand to one of bamboo poles, to make the ivory tea scoop of bamboo and to change the flower container from Chinese copper to one made of bamboo. Shuko was unable to achieve this ideal during his lifetime because of his employment by the military dictator Yoshimasa. But he nevertheless discussed it with his pupil, Shutoku, who gradually advanced preparations towards the ideal.

Yet when he died Shuko's ideal was brought to a halt because of the long continued disruption of war. Thereafter people who loved peace and enjoyed cultured pursuits left the area of Kyoto and moved to peaceful and habitable areas.

A man of tea called Takeno Jo-o also left Kyoto at that time to live in Sakai. He was the tea man who can be said to have completed the simple and natural tea ceremony in a grass hut that had been Shuko's ideal.

The expression 'simple and natural' comes from the word 'wabi' which is the noun formed from the verb 'wabu'. This word was used in literature since antiquity for a feeling of discontent and forlorn anxiety. It often appears in the Manyoshu, Kokinshu and other anthologies, but with the establishment of the way of poetry it became ·a poetic ideal in itself. Jo-o interpreted it as follows: 'wabi' is a word which those now passed on recited in various poems. It has also recently become genuinely circumspect in its usage and means an inextravagant appearance'. He thus interprets wabi as being satisfied with deficiency and behaving with circusmpection.

Accordingly, Jo-o avoided the tea ceremonies in a reception room which were in the taste of the nobility. He made a tea hall by cutting a hole for the brazier in a four and a half mat room, which was straw-roofed in imitation of a peasant house. In place of tea utensils of the 'Chinese things' variety, he used salt and seed jars fired in Bizen and Seto, and Shiga-raki ware as tea ceremony utensils. He selected tea bowls, tea containers and water jars from a variety of general vessels in everday use.

Thus the tea ceremony came to place greater emphasis on the

participant's frame of mind than on either the utensils employed or the place where it took place. The tea ceremony which had simply been an aristocratic pastime and a social courtesy grew into the way upheld by the spirit of wabi, so much so that it could be entitled the Way of Tea.

Sen no Rikyu

Sen no Rikyu was a pupil of Takeno Jo-o who was born in Sakai in 1522. Rikyu studied under Jo-o until the latter's death in 1555 at the age of 53. During the approximately 15 years Rikyu received instruction as Jo-o's pupil, he underwent Zen instruction at Shunoku and Kokei in Daitoku-ji Temple, and endeavoured to grasp the spirit of the way of tea. He also went on travels to various areas, was taught by the heads of pottery kilns, and refined his original ideas for new tea vessels.

In 1578, when he was aged 58, Rikyu was summoned by Oda Nobunaga and added to his following. However, when Nobunaga died in 1582, he was once again taken into the service of Nobunaga's successor, Hideyoshi, and was given a stipend of three thousand bushels of rice.

It may be noted that Hideyoshi was already by that time famous as a great tea man. We may ask why he should have given Rikyu, an ordinary townsman of Sakai, this kind of high salary and have employed him in his close entourage. It was because Hideyoshi intended to try to use the way of tea in the reconciliation of warriors and townspeople, to soften the hearts of discontented ordinary people who had been downcast since the time of the warring countries, and the hearts of unrefined generals who had grown wild and dissolute. Rikyu fully co-operated in this scheme of Hideyoshi's, who himself also enjoyed the way of tea. When Hideyoshi had a little free time he tried to find space to relax in the tea room, where he drank the tea

Rikyu prepared.

Accordingly, Rikyu always went with Hideyoshi to his battlefields. The present 'Tai-an' two mat tea house at Myoki-an, Yamazaki, Kyoto Prefecture, which is designated as an Important Cultural Property, was built by Rikyu as a place of relaxation for Hideyoshi at the time of the Battle of Yamazaki. This narrow tea house was Rikyu's idea who thought that if the room was small, the mind would not be distracted, and that if one sat here, the heart would be composed even in the middle of a fierce battle.

On the 7th of October, 1585, Hideyoshi held his first tea party in the Imperial Palace, when a special seat was also assigned Rikyu on whom the imperial title of Rikyu Koji–'Layman of Buddhism'– was specially conferred. The appellation Soeki had been used earlier, but Rikyu was used from then on. The name comes from a Zen phrase and means 'without esteem or riches'.

The future gulf now opened between Rikyu and Hideyoshi. As Rikyu advanced in years he carried out his way of tea with and increasingly profound feeling of wabi. Hideyoshi in opposition to this separated from the wabi interpreted by Rikyu. For example, Rikyu was fascinated by the fisherman's creel employed in fishing on the Katsura river and used it as a flower container. He himself cut bamboo and made the tea scoops and flower containers he utilised in the tea ceremony. Hideyoshi, however, built a tea room with walls of gold leaf and triumphantly had all the tea vessels made of gold. This was the essence of Hideyoshi's way of tea, whereas the essence of that employed by Rikyu's wabi tea was perhaps to be found in the objective of gaining popularity with ordinary citizens.

Eventually Hideyoshi was annoyed by Rikyu who displayed the attitude of a saint and preached the spirit of simplicity in

112

◀ Sen no Rikyu

all things. Hideyoshi soon concluded there was no longer any want of Rikyu. On the 25th of February 1591 he ordered the death of Rikyu for treason. On the 28th of February, after leaving a farewell poem, Rikyu killed himself with his own sword and so ended a lifetime of seventy years.

Rikyu's way of tea had more profoundly entered the spirit of wabi than that of Jo-o. For, in contrast to the secluded wabi of Jo-o, Rikyu's wabi had in the stillness concealed a new vitality. Such a philosophy of wabi was quite relevant to the people of the time who were rich in vitality.

Rikyu also made various improvements in the variety of tea vessels. Those which had come from China, called 'Chinese things', had for example been prized up until Rikyu's time, but he had tea bowls fired to his own design by the potters brought back from Korea. This was Raku ware. He also had flower containers fired in Seto, Bizen and so forth. He discovered vessels he could use as tea bowls and water jars among the everyday things brought by the people who came from Korea to work in Japan. This was rather than use vessels imported from abroad, even such tea bowls with the beautifully finished shape of celadon or blue and white.

Apart from these, there were not a few vessels such as the ~~lantern used by fishermen or well buckets~~ which were adopted as tea vessels because of his unsurpassed aesthetic sense. Aside from the tea stand, the only shelf used in the preparation of tea had been the bag shelf liked by Jo-o, but Rikyu preferred the small size shelf variety because such shelves as used by Jo-o were too large a size for the small tea room. Tea vessels not withstanding he devised leather soled sandals and horse trappings, and even such things as sword sheaths were brought about by his simple and unaffected spirit. These innovations made a great contribution to the development of Japanese ceramics and crafts.

The way of tea after Rikyu's death

Rikyu had two children. The first, by his earlier wife, was called Doan. The second child, who he adopted, was brought in marriage by his later wife, So-on, and was called Shoan. Shoan's child, Sotan, was given to Daitoku-ji Temple as an infant where he devoted himself to Zen austerities. But when Sotan was fifteen or sixteen he went to live with his father, Shoan, who had retired to the Shonan pavilion he had built in the Saiho-ji Temple on Nishiyama.

Sotan was educated by Rikyu's later wife, So-on, who was a rarely seen woman of high culture. It was with this woman that Sotan spent his youth and through her that he received direction in every aspect of the way of tea. Because Sotan was the third head of the Sen household, that is the Senke School of tea, there were invitations for Sotan to be taken into the service of the Tokugawa family and the local feudal lords as their official tea master. He never conceded to these requests because even in his heart as a child, he had strongly felt that his grandfather, Rikyu, had been forced to comply with his own death sentence for having been given a stipend by Hideyoshi.

He may well have believed that the spirit of wabi could not be born in a golden tea room or in the feudal lord's luxurious way of life, and that the spirit of Rikyu's way should first be brought to life among ordinary citizens to whom it belonged. Sotan consequently lived a life of poverty whilst carrying the burden of the revival of the Senke school. It is if only in this austere way of life that Sotan's heart of tea gradually reached into wabi. Moreover, the philosophy of Zen which had been built up in him through austerities since infancy complemented his tea to the extent that it could be called 'Zen and Tea in one flavour'.

At the age of 71 Sotan completed a tea house called 'Konnichi-an' to which he retired. He passed on the Fushin-an, in which he had hitherto lived, to his third son Sosa, which was thereafter called Omote Senke of Front Senke school. Sotan's fourth son, Soshitsu, moved to the Konnichi-an with his father, which was called the Ura Senke or Rear Senke school. Because the two sons had each set up their own houses, the second son, Soshu, himself also took the name of the district in which he was living on the Mushanokoji river and named his household Mushanokoji Senke, whose representative tea-house was called the 'Kankyu-an'.

Sen Sotan ▶

After the death of Rikyu, the way of tea thus split into the three households or schools of Omote Senke, Ura Senke and Mushanokoji Senke, at the time of his grandson Sotan.

There were many different schools created in the middle of the Edo period, most of which may be said to have been further divided from the three Senke Schools. It can be argued that many schools came about because of an increase in people learning the way of tea.

The way of tea in the Edo period

A feudal system which centralized authority was established by the Tokugawa military government. With the fixing of personal status into the four ranks of warrior, farmer, craftsman and merchant, regulations of service were also established for men of tea. They were separated into the classes of head of the tea pavilion, tea master, tea priest and so forth as teachers to the military dictator's household in Edo castle. A stipend was given to each of these ranks. The great feudal lords throughout the country themselves practised the military government's system and called tea men into their service. Tea men were thus professionalized and, with the establishment of their own class, they were pressed by the need to find the qualifications which would give them status.

Whilst tea became popular with the military government and feudal lords, it also flourished among the townspeople. Merchants in particular used the tea ceremony in commercial negotiations with the feudal lords, and the holding of tea meetings and tea occasions increased for this reason.

Confucianism suddenly rose to power from the middle of the end of the Edo period. It was made use of by the military government and thus Buddhism declined, for it had hitherto been protected by the influence of the government. In consequence, the way of tea, which had largely been within the Buddhist current of thought, was oppressed by the power of Confucians, and tea men also met a poor reception. At this point tea men sought to extend their own influence with the economically prosperous townspeople as their object.

From the Meiji period to the present day

Japan was eventually opened up with the end of military rule. With the age of the liberalization of culture, the pattern of the tea ceremony, which had up to then a strongly feudal colouring, lost the interest of the ordinary masses, and the way of tea temporarily arrived at a period of recession. Moreover, the tea men had lived securely with their feudal status, and had been teachers all along of a stereo typed etiquette. They were unable to trim their sails to the winds of the times and this recession was an adversity they did not overcome.

The head of the Ura Senke school, Gengensai Soshitsu, was one of those tea men. But he worked to adjust the rules of tea to the new age with the creative impulse he applied in the 'upright eituqette' of 1872, which he devised for preparing tea on a table with chairs.

A 'National Thought' movement arose at the time of the Russo-Japanese and Sino-Japanese wars. The spirit of the way of tea was re-examined and a prosperous era reached again for the tea ceremony. The Senke way of tea, which had the oldest tradition and was moreover comparatively the richest in creativity, surpassed the other schools. Its revived influence continues today.

The way of tea since the Meiji period has not been the snobbish thing it was at the end of the Edo period. It has been democratised so that a liking for its elegant tastes can be formed by the ordinary masses, but in its place there is also the feeling it has been stereotyped and turned into a business. Teachers of the tea ceremony were limited to men until the Meiji period. But with its popularization more women than men have learnt the tea ceremony and the number of women teachers has therefore increased. Even though this has not been considered a problem until now in theoretical studies of the tea ceremony, in historical investigation, and in the appreciation of tea vessels and so forth, the issue has now begun to be put forward among scholars and connoisseurs.

II. ON THE WAY OF TEA

When Rikyu was asked by a certain pupil, 'What are the secrets of the Way of Tea?', Rikyu replied that 'There are seven secrets. Make the tea so that your guest will enjoy it; place charcoal so that it will boil water; arrange the flower in a way suited to it; keep the atmosphere of the tea room cool in summer and warm in winter; be ahead of time; prepare an umbrella even if no rain falls; attune your heart to the other guests.'

These words, together with the four rules of Harmony, Reverance, Purity and Tranquility (Wa Kei Sei Jaku) are Rikyu's 'Four Rules and Seven Principles' which must always remain in the heart of someone learning the way of tea.

The four rules interpret the spirit of the man of tea, the seven principles teach the frame of mind when encountering other people.

1. When making a cup of tea to be drunk by a guest, it is more important to make drinkable and pleasant tea that to pay attention to the etiquette of preparation. It must not be forgotten that to put one's heart into making tea is more important than the suitability of the utensils or the relative skill in tea preparation. This is not only limited to tea, for one should not be obsessed by form and convention and above all one should not forget the heart, when meeting people and in one's work.

2. There is an etiquette for preparing charcoal in the way of tea. Even though it is only for boiling water, an etiquette has been laid down for replenishing fuel in

the brazier and portable brazier. Whilst there is an etiquette and there are rules, the purpose of replenishing charcoal is to boil water, so this should be done so that the water boils quickly. There is therefore no need to replenish fuel according to the rules, just because a rule says so, if there is plenty of charcoal left. Consider what will make the water boil quickly. This will also eliminate wastage.

3. The flower in the tea room is arranged in a way suitable to it, not by proportioning its form or by senselessly bending its twigs, but by arranging the shape as it would be in nature. This is not only true of arranging flowers. The way of tea respects the unadorned truth. Isn't the enjoyment of a natural appearance without its over-sophistication also important in our everyday life?

4. Keep the atmosphere of the tea room cool in summer and warm in winter indicates an attitude which does not go against nature.

5. Being ahead of time indicates that it is best to have a frame of mind where one is always a little earlier than the promised time. The principle of being on time has come to be widely observed at present, but it is better to go early leaving a little time in hand before the exact hour. It is also desirable in our daily lives to always have a little time to spare rather than do everything at the last moment.

6. Prepare an umbrella even if no rain falls is not only limited to rain and snow. It indicates that the heart should always be ready for any untoward change.

7. Attune your heart to the other guests, indicates that one does not live in human society as if only one's

own feelings mattered. One must act in full consideration for other people.

The seven principles also teach several things about everyday
life outside the way of tea which we are forced to consider. In
the way of tea we acquire such a spirit through preparing tea and
becoming a guest.

When life becomes restless we seek the quietness of things
and beg for time to think. If etiquette is abused, ceremonious
deportment will be thought beautiful. The way of tea is therefore still essential today. But it is not only a way inside the tea
room. Its purpose can be attained in the future because
its spirit will revitalise our daily lives.

INDEX

(This index does not include items given on the contents page.)

HOIKUSHA COLOR BOOKS

ENGLISH EDITIONS

Book Size 4″×6″

COLORED ILLUSTRATIONS FOR NATURALISTS

Text in Japanese, with index in Latin or English.

Book Size 6″ × 8″

SHELLS
OF
THE
WESTERN
PACIFIC
IN
COLOR

Book Size 7″×10″

⟨vol. I⟩ by Tetsuaki Kira
(304 pages, 72 in color)
⟨vol. II⟩ by Tadashige Habe
(304 pages, 66 in color)

FISHES
OF
JAPAN
IN
COLOR

Book Size 7″×10″

by Toshiji Kamohara
(210 pages, 64 in color)